Once Upon A Heartbreak

Tawanda Chitewe

Published by Tawanda Chitewe, 2024.

ONCE UPON A HEARTBREAK

First edition. September 6, 2024.

ISBN: 979-8227460844

Written by Tawanda Chitewe.

For the boy I was and the husband I have become.

Game no Eke!

ONCE UPON A HEARTBREAK

AN ANTHOLOGY
BY
TAWANDA CHITEWE

ACKNOWLEDGEMENTS

To my wonderful wife, this is the chaos that plagued my love life before you saved me.

BIOGRAPHY

Born on January 17, 1990, in Harare, Zimbabwe, Tawanda Chitewe is a talented poet and writer who has been weaving words into verse since 2008. With a passion for storytelling and a keen eye for detail, he has honed his craft over the years, exploring themes of identity, love, culture, and the human experience.

Through his poetry, Tawanda offers a unique perspective on the world, drawing inspiration from his heritage and the complexities of modern life. With a voice both authentic and evocative, he continues to captivate readers and audiences alike, solidifying his place as a rising star in the literary world.

pg.

SEARCHING

"It is not right for a man or woman to be alone. Try as you may to deny it, we all have that innate desire for companionship. Whether you end up finding it in another human being, religion, a pet, or an activity, the goal is the same. We are completed by something more than just ourselves"

My Lady

Listen! Obi Mu is about to speak.
Like Adam in the garden, I am one of a kind
But Alas! Alone in a paradise created
Where is my companion?

    Where is my Eve?

A Sarah to this Abraham is what I need
A blessing to the womb of my heart
One I would feel ripen
In an age when all hope seems lost
Is possible to find my Sarah?

    Where is my Sarah?

If not, then Ruth come give me proof
That women like you do exist
That you are not confined to the mind's construction
Please come forth, make me believe
That love like yours is not a myth

    Where is my Ruth?

I need one like Hannah to call my wife
A prayer warrior whose faith in God will never cease
So compassionate, understanding, and grateful
Standing by her promise
She gave back her Samuel

    Where is my Hannah?

Where is the one with a heart like Esther?
Whose words and advocacy will bring salvation
Words that bring life and not destruction
So bold and confident she will bring forth justice
Save a people, save a nation.

Where is my Esther?

Love is Blind

They say love is blind
Maybe that's why I can't find it.
The long fruitless search
Now I'm beginning to mind it.
Listen!
Mine is now ripe and ready,
As if about to burst
With cancerous cells of emotional résumés.
I wish you could fathom the breath of it all
The need to be one with the heart,
Beat!
Of another.
Before mine starts fading in the blue horizon over yonder.
Would you answer the phone for me when the call comes through?
Beckoning me to answer while my hands are stuck together like glue.
Or would you sit back, relax, recline, and laugh?
Find joy in my implosive contemplation.
I wonder?
I know that love is blind
That's why I can't find it
But though it may be blind I know I should at least feel it.

Spoken

I speak more of what could be
Because I am not entirely
The self I would become
Till I find what I seek.
Imprinted on the fore of the
Heart I store is the urge to grow
And cascade down the walls
Of the ever-green meadows
That belch like violins and cellos
Screamin Juliet! Juliet!
Where art thou my Juliet?
In a place where reality finally
Made peace with my lady fantasy.
The self I would become
When I find what I seek
Would be like the day the wife meets
Her husband from that horrible war
An explosion of jovial emotional confusion
Expressed by the tears
Once wiped off with fear
Now flooding the streets
With the words 'Oh Dear!'
The self I would become
When I find what I seek
Would be like the first rains
In the barren land
Which consumes the parched earth
Clobbering the cracks away
Making way for the daisies and lilies
at bay

Paving the way for the lush laurel to
Flourish
It's a shame, it all seems a myth
The self I'll become now seems so bleak
But I'll stand firm in my boat when the lake dries up
And when all the fish in the
Sea go upstream for summer
Chasing after the Lockness
Such a horrible contest.
My eye remains glued on the lone tree in the orchard,
For its time to bear fruit now brings
Forth the spring
And the time for my heart to hold

Firm and believe.

In Love

"Love is a beautiful thing best appreciated and enjoyed when shared with others. Most of us remember what it was like when we felt the butterflies fluttering in our stomachs for the first time. Most of us remember our first crush and the feeling upon discovering that the feelings were mutual. Wasn't that magical? Then again, there were times when the other person didn't feel the same. Do you recall what that felt like?"

Love

On the playground, you would hear us sing
He loves you, no, he loves you not
She loves me or she loves me not.
Love!
And in the classroom
You would hear my teacher blurt
Noun love – *a strong positive emotion of regard and affection*
Verb love make- *have sexual intercourse with*
Verb love – *get pleasure from*
Love
L.O.V.E
Why can't SHE see me?
Through all these inside-the-box definitions I still stand here as ME
With no rose to replace the rib Eve took.
Fortified in these words
Is the blatant plea for the phoenix approach to this
Intangible gold-encrusted diamond cashmere Cloak my heart desires.
LOVE!
To rendezvous with it on neutral ground
And sign the treaty that would dispose of the
mountains, mounds, and rugged terrains that seduced the sand
Forming a Sahara between me and Her
LOVE!
Verb, LOVE, to make love.
No intercourse of course but a mere
Plea to flee from this Kalahari of dry tears
That leaves grains in the closet
Far from where She can see
The ten thousand grains for all the days that I have cried for Her
LOVE.

Make love not war
But on cupids arrow I'll call upon the friendly foe
To neutralize my heart before it implodes
But alas, I am no Shaka Zulu
All I have is a LOVE letter for a shield and assegai-shaped words for you
my dear
But she chooses to wait for the rain
Like Charles Mungoshi
Far from my fire
Far from the defined noun of warm affection.
LOVE!
LOVE is patient and love is kind
But what kind is the kind that fills the cavity of my chest
For patience now feels like a framework of passivity?
Verb, Love
Get pleasure from what?
When she calls you friend?
And on your heart she plays tennis
With her exe like the woodsman
With the umpire screaming out
One love
Upon every stroke and count
The defeat encased in a Trojan horse.
If Love were a 'him' would she love him too?
And if love were a hymn, would she sing it too?
Serenade to each other the sweet melodies of compassion
While I choke at this awful dreaded fear of being left alone and forgotten
by
LOVE.

Beautiful

Watch as the braid is pulled back
With such elegance
As if dancing to the tune of the warm summer breeze.
Listen to that adorable endearing smile crack that smooth finespun natural skin
Lightly pronounced by a dash of freckles
Gently polished by Mother Nature's nurturing touch
Like an interlude, she stands out with her very own unequaled strand of beauty
One in sync with mind, body, and spirit
One placid and paralleled by no manly figure
Her cohesive beauty I so admire.
For a jewel like her, I would gladly brace the raging currents of all the seven seas
In a quest to relax in the heart of the one whose beauty I could never fathom
Capricious and fulgurous
My pupils dilate when I see her smile
Her entrancing beauty I admire
Our whimsical encounter had me glaring in wonder
At the apple, the flower of my God-given eyes
Dumbstruck, stupified, and flabbergasted was I
Like 'Little Boy Blue' with a cookie or two.
You invaded my heart while I, like Adam lay in slumber
The creation of humanity redefined
And incarnated in the form of a fairer sex in my quiescent state
Her flawless beauty I so admire
The eyes, the lips, the fruits the hips
All congregate on such a divine masterpiece
Attention to detail and laconic

Surely He had me at heart
When molding the vessel that would conceive and usher in new life into
this world
Her enchanting beauty I so admire.
Suave beauty legato from head to toe.
Beautiful you, need I ask for more
Rather let the Twist in my heart remain in an alcove
And let my eye gaze in wonder
For it is a price I'm willing to pay
For her enthralling beauty which I so deeply admire.
Now watch as that beauty seeps through the pores of her golden
effulgent skin
As if drawn in by some dire need to embed it in a place where only the
heart can see
Listen to her soul speak volumes of inner perfection
Luring the self into a trance of satisfaction
Surely she is and forever will be my beautiful.

Eden

Your eyes will see a piece of land
And lust for its prolificacy,
Its fruits.
For its wonders, you will gaze upon them with awe
Your cornea will shimmer
As the craving grows deeper.
Whether owned or not
Your need will not wither.
For when intentions are noble
Your heart leads the way.
Dear land! The conquer note would read
I come in peace, to orison my request to occupy you
At the heart of your meadow.
For if violets are blue
My interest is true
To help end this wonderer's life the pith lives.
Take me into thy comfort zone
And let me rest my head on thy valley thyrse.
A dove as white as snow
Carries the petition to the core
But a falcon arises and slays the medium
One after the other they all fall like dominos.
And as if feeding the land,
Its core flourishes more and more.
Syphoning the life out of the wonderer's pith
Watch it shrivel!
Watch as the field once deemed paradise
Hurl javelins at every medium put to use.
It moves not its leaves nor ruffles its streams
Nor move its mountains for a glimpse of its enchanted center.

It is there within sight
But far from the traveler's reach.
You will die of thirst
Weep but not shed a single tear
But granules of parched particles
As your heart bleeds for her lush green grass.
Defy the laws of physics you may
Obscure the sun from shinning the light of day
But engrave your name on a heart that beats a different tune
Is like rolling a boulder to heaven.
Like sands through the hourglass
So will the love inside of you depart
Like a slow death through a life whose spark finds appeasement
In a fantasy that does not suffice.
No need to ponder!
Open your eyes and see
That your own lush terrain is only a garden shed away
By faith and perseverance, you will have your own
EDEN!

And if

So many times I have peeped through the classroom door
Hid behind the library bookshelves
Just to gaze upon your angelic glow.
So many times I have printed your name on the covers of my journals
Rehearsed the words that would have you say "I DO"
And if you let me in the confines of your heart
To plant that seed of ever-lasting smiles
I'll paint a picture so vivid
That will have Cloud 9 descend
I come before you as a sculptor
And if you let me in your heart
I'll carve a fountain of joy at the center of its marrow
So it may ooze and overflow to all nooks and corners that split the joy
from its core.
So it may consume the little dark gremlins of past pains and deceit
From the Alibabas that ransacked
The love from your heart
I come before you as a philosopher
To redefine the meaning of love
For what I have is no dose of infatuation or eros
But the romantic philia with a dose of agape
As coined by the Platos and Aristostles of ages that passed.
To hold your hand with care and compassion
As we take baby steps in our newfound love.
And if you let me love you
I would love you till the end of time
Even when the last breath is exhaled from my earthly vessel
A replay that would recall in my dormant state
Would be a rehearsal of the love il show you in the life to come
Yes it's true

The love I have for you has grown so strong that reincarnation would be
by its hand
And if you let me love you
I surely won't waste your time
For you have the spark I can not ignore
Beauty I would give tribute and praise to
And when its all said and done
And your heart is mine
I'll have you as my wife
My companion for life.
So let US be for you to see
How great life can become when it's just you and me
When we glide on petals floating in the mid-summer breeze
And listen to each other's heartbeat as we waltz
Glued to each other's eyes
When we carve our names on the swings and Jacaranda trees
And blow kisses at each other through little notes and letters
Such wonderful times to come.
I present to you my heart
Will I have yours in return?

Falling

She is like that lone oasis in the middle of the desert
That seeks to quench the traveler's thirst
And gives shade to the sweat that breaks off his brow
Have him relax in the comfort of its splendor.
She is like that break of dawn from a night of pain and anguish
That had one bound in chains of introspective self pitty
Watch her bring forth the key to unshackling the self
Watch her come forth like the gentle summer rain
To wash away the African scorch from my parched heart
And finally, watch her descend like an angel, so complete and perfect
To save my soul from the pain I could never bear.
Watch me sore in the clouds way above level nine
In the comfort of her majesty's wings
For she has conquered my heart with her love.
She has become my royal damsel, smothering me with joy.
Let the earth feel my jovial tears rain like a tsunami
Flooding the streets, alleys, valleys and plains
From the depths of my heart
For the fountain will never exsiccate.
Yes! Let them feel the beat of my gladdened heart
Echo like war drums from battles of eras that passed.
And so I explode into this whole new person
This feeling, this feeling that has gripped me
Feels like taking a glimpse of heaven
For my haven now lies in her amazing self
She has me falling
No rather tumbling
Right into her compassionate embrace.
Her smile awakens the butterflies in my stomach
As I let it entice my youth into a frenzy of appeasement

I LOVE this girl so much.
Reason why she has become my heart's companion
Reason why I boast and brag about her.
Reason why I will move mountains, heaven, and earth
To have her close to my chest
So our hearts can beat as one.

Forbidden Love

A notion scripted in an orthodox order
Restrict the pith like a trammel
To dwell at the center of a brand-new sun.
Caged in, locked in, locked out!
The sting of unempowered contemplation.
The sting of taking no action.
The sting of forbidden Love
Like a light at the break of dawn, you will see her, carrying the evening
sorrows back into the termite mounds where they belong.
And like the burdened morning grass disembarrassed
One's smile will stand tall and bold
Like a Marula tree, openly inviting
The life she brings.
But orison a letter to her majesty the damsel One dares not
The thud of the judge's hammer One fears most
For inscribed expectations dictate
That a union should never, ever manifest.
Like dying of thirst while afloat on a raft!
The shore is near, but the market ale you do not fancy
The shore is clear, but her maidens your heart ignores
Why did we have to be leased together in the same place of chores?
Roses grow beneath my feet,
Some attempting to trip and topple the strides taken towards the echo of
your voice
You have morphed me into a victim of your paragon persona
So now like a zombie, I am helplessly drawn
To the form that shines so brightly,
I am a moth to a light
But then again the foreman walks in
And my mind is ignited into a frenzy of reasons why we could never be

Reasons beyond my reach, both night and day
Palm and chin will meet again tonight
And converse over how I struggled to keep my eyes off you
The mouth will whisper to the feet below
About how they orchestrated the event that had one standing before
you, completely devoid of letters or vowels
To utter in your presence.
The only option is to secretly admire
The girl in whom hopes of a happier union reside.
It is hard to feel like this again after a hurricane
Even harder to ignore and let it torment you over and over again.
The thorn in my flesh!
But if fate would have it and our paths crossed
Would You let me hold you close?

The Girl in the Purple Dress

As calm as the breeze after the storm
She has restored peace to a life once left in shambles
And as if she were daughter to the sun
She has ushered in warmth on the cloudiest of days
Piercing through their thick misery with ease
Her smile has firmly rooted itself in my heart
I can see it every single time I close my eyes.
Ambushed by her beauty and her persona
I, like a feather, floated into a deep trance
Fueled by fantasies of what she and I would achieve.
Like a ten-foot-long ancient scroll
I would unroll infinite reasons why I would make her mine
And as if blessed by the spirit of a thousand tongues
I would confess my affection in every tongue known to man
Over and over again.
And when she would wear that purple dress
In a trance, I would once again float.
To hear that another has caused her to frown
Caused her to sulk or even made her cry
I would unleash a fury greater than any Egyptian army
Defend her honour I would, till my last breath.
If I could, I would hide her in the deepest corner of my heart
So that any weapon fashioned against her
Would only reach its mark after going through me.
I would lay down my life,
Forsake my own happiness
For the girl in the purple dress

Magnetic

A moth to light, no strength to fight
The desire that brews in the coldest night
Reform and ignite, the fire inside
Open the doors and let love decide.
Hush now, Obi Mu is about to speak!
Scarred by the ignorance of its infancy
Mistakes sealed in a layer of moth and rust
The cracks and bruises foretell a brutal past
One in which promises and oaths engraved in stone
Became the ravenous projectiles that clobbered its flesh and bone.
Now battered and bruised it feard to commit
Entry to its core it would never permit.
Behold, she rises in the east like the sun
Her warmth weakening the frost that had once been spun
Drawing him closer to her, self like a magnet
From her gravitational pull, he can never run.
The warmth reviving, seeping into each fragment
And unlocking the doors that lead to his heart
Watch him hand it over with an open palm
A moth to light, no strength to fight
The desire that brews in the coldest night
Reform and ignite, the fire inside

Watch him surrender his heart to her tonight.

The Storm

"Some say that nothing hurts more than having the one you truly love break your heart. We have all loved at some point in our lives. Do you remember how you felt when it started? Was there ever a time when expressing your love was all you could think about? When you gave it your all, at times even losing yourself in the process? Then you understand fully the pain of having that very same person break your heart. Whether slowly through gradual personality changes or incompatibility or maybe sudden discoveries that shocked you senseless"

Flaws of Attraction

If humans were ruled by emotions
Who would reign over the emotions?
And if we all bowed down and gave into our weakness
Would we ever be able to reclaim our glory?
Here is the tear that will soon disappear in the sand.
Where were your emotions when your heart was ambushed?
'Unlike poles attract', they say
But collide and explode they often do
Like using dynamite to light the night,
Close your ears so you can at least see it coming your way.
The love shot down like a grouse off-season.
Ten virgins or more will salivate for your saintly virtues
But ignore them you shall
For the harlot next door.
He will give you his heart, his armor, his all,
But you will reply him with an arrow
That pierces beyond the soul.
Neon lights will flicker, pointing in her direction
But you will stay glued to the hungry dragon's breath,
With an infatuated mindset.
The hex of flawed laws of attraction.
Engage, disengage, separate, long for.
Falling for the one that will flee from you
Is like the error-ridden attempts
To fit in jig saw pieces that fail to connect.
Roses are red
And violets are blue,
Even Romeo and Juliet never saw it through.
The emotional pilgrimage has failed us thus far.
What say you to this paradox conundrum?

The Question

Am I ...walking through these streets and forsaking the sweet beat of the heart that skips

At every thought of me as I...with my two feet walk right by

Do I... recognize the frame and not the picture

Water the vase and not the flower

While I...focus on the mustard seed of discontent sown by the seemingly passive dissonance in I

Should I...stop this introspective memoir

This continuous pondering upon my interior war

Pause

Was she a rebound long overdue???

Because due to this feeling that no longer holds dew

The need arises to salvage a few

Thoughts and memories to hold this back in place like glue

Lest it exfoliates in the absence of screws.

And now I...think like a banana, change colour, and split

Make like an elephant and never jump the broom

But fly like Jumbo I let my imagination wander

Into places, my heart starts beating fonder.

Reflection

I tried to plant love in a place where it would never grow
Amongst thorns and hoards of stones that would tumble and fall.
And placed it on a rigid wooden white ant-infested, gnarled stage.
The mission was to seek, claim, impress, and conquer
The heart of a damsel in whichever form.
Look, I really meant well!
I really did mean to save her and I from the well.
But fate would have it that infatuation would subside
And have reason prevail, at par with sanity
All of which I had suppressed with the iron fist of self-imposed obligation
Weaved together like feathers and wax.
In my prologue to breaking a girl's heart.
I did fly!
Right on top of a lava pool of 'what were you thinking?'
And like an overripe fruit from a tree, it all came crashing down
Like bird droppings on a wedding gown.
Now I caused a girl to cry
And she still wonders why
I would let myself deceive us both.
Though the fault is definitely not all mine
I rue the day I planted the seed
That only sprouted and mothered weeds.
That tangled up till they broke a girl's heart!
An apology now will not suffice
Even though you and I did share a thousand smiles
You played your part in this childish chared
Your stage show was by far personified perfection
So good that even you have been numbed in sight.
Bravo!

But still...I helped break a girl's heart
Square one is where I recline and introspect like a prisoner saved from
the deathly gallows
Never to repeat such an atrocity again,
Never to be the grim reaper of joy,
The harvester of happiness,
The breaker of hearts.
But taking time to recollect and reflect
On other fields to nurture the seed
In hopes that it would one day
Blossom into a tree of never-ending compliments
For making a girl smile

Repent

Even the blind can see
That my campus is broken
That wooden stakes protrude from my ears' drum
That the recoils from past endeavors now make me numb
The deaf can hear the 'ME' cry out
For a sober beginning, they hear the 'I' scream out
The Morris code they hear my heart tap out
Like a telegram they all have their pens dash out
For the message now tells the tale of the sun that has set searching for my smile
Searching for the glow that brightens its show
Even the moon now cries for its long-lost philia
Once perpetuated by my fondest muscle
The one I call cardiac, the one they arrested
As straight as an arrow blown off course by the wind
The target now drifts away so bleak
As to hit anything of substance
No longer matters
When the essence behind the arrow falls short of the target's predetermined calibrated position
Unwavering!
Now let me recuperate
Enough has been said already.
Through a word, a caption, a statement a phrase
A series of words that spell out DISMAY.
Painted in black and brown
Even immortals will feel the rigid thread
As it sows the muscle in efforts to mend
That thing that the psyche failed to defend
Though now I pretend

I still see no end
The arrow continues to twirl and bend
Until alas the last gasp whispers
REPENT!

Sixteen

16 times or more she has crawled to the door
Trying to flee from the incessant barrage of your fists and limbs
16 times or more you have wiped the sweat from your forehead
With the remaining strands of hair in your hand
Tangled in its grim vain filled stiffness
From the pulling and tugging of her head
While you beat her down to the size of a pulp
16 times or more like a recurring encore
16 times or more she has begged you to stop
But you, remaining resolute in your vile endeavor
Unleash your legion of devastation on her fragile body
The one you choose not to handle with care.
Now 16 scars or more emerge like cracks and crevices on exfoliating rock
While she becomes a punching bag 16 hours or more round the clock.
16 times or more your words have destroyed him like a town in the path
of a collapsed dam wall
As with 16 tongues or more, you emasculate him with 16 words plus
more.
And if need be you have smacked him in the head with a rolling pin
Scolded his face with some molten lava oil
Or bit his flesh to get the message clear
Leaving 16 tooth marks if not more
16 times or more your neighbors have slept with wooden stakes in their
ears
To drown that verbal battle you so frequently partake in
Before 16 screams or more echo through the corridor from your children
Trying to restrain the devil in you from shedding more blood.
But on 16 occasions if not more you turned on those innocent souls
And laid 16 slaps and more till their bodies became disfigured with
bruises

On 16 spots or more.
But 16 days have shown how a people can end this war
Through 16 words of apology or less
Or when 16 men and women or more
Come together with 16 sensible reasons if not more
To act against gender-based violence
Through 16 days or more of the white ribbon
16 smiles or more will become our future
LET'S ACT TOGETHER AGAINST GENDER-BASED VIOLENCE.

The Inevitable End

"All things must come to an end, and accepting this is accepting wisdom. Fight as hard as you can, but the fact remains, that all things must come to an end. Not that you should live in constant fear. No! Rather use this knowledge to make the most of the little time given to each of us with something or someone we love. And when the end comes, don't hold back your tears, rather weep, mourn, or cry with the future in mind"

Heartache Smile

The mind deprived of its right to smile
Is like a heart deprived and devoid of love
A dove with no feathers
A command with no letters or vowels
Like quick without the silver
An angel with no wings
Clipped by the notoriously menacing evil of man.
Should men forget and abandon the race?
Make up for the head start,
The ambush contains?
As it weaves through the cardiac muscle
Forcing its way through every stroke
As it brings decay.
The unseemingly lifeless end to life,
Whose contrast rose the beauty from her sleep.
Now listen closely!
Do you hear the heart, break?
Because I can, from the face of the host
Who at most never thought they could bear the cost and even find the
words lost when they exclaimed I DO!
Interject that thought with the sad love story
And rewind the plot to its day of glory
And that warm fuzzy feeling
When you and I became US!
Though past I still long so much
For the tale to be rewritten on a plate of glass
And engraved on the heart that now
Defines my pain
Dont flatter karma with the words
'I'm sorry'

Just move on and hover like the dark cloud
You have become

Unbecoming

The prophecy written on these walls has always been shrouded in mystery,
Only making sense upon fulfillment.
Words, like cement, hold the bricks together for the architectural structure
Binding what is to come in an indestructible form,
One that holds the secrets of the fate that is yet to manifest
And become reality.
Decisions, suggestions, and contemplations we make
Paths we may deviate from, but not the goals set before us,
For the fulfillment of fate and destiny will always come to pass.
Inextricably bound to what is to become of you.
No matter how hard you stare at it in the beginning,
The picture will only become clearer at the very end.
Like a child born with such great expectations,
Do not despise them for the delinquent they become in the end,
Unacceptable, So unbecoming!
If not them, then WHO?
Was it not the fate bestowed on them even before you were formed?
Was it not a fair allotment according to the needs of a well-balanced society?
Whose plain features the eye can never
Indulge in and remain delighted.
Fact or point to ponder and clobber.
Listen! The walls speak in a deep baritone voice,
"Time is the only acceptable medium of exchange!"
Time reveals the inscriptions
Why so many of them broke your heart before you met "THE ONE"
Why you never got to say goodbye
Why you could never let go

Why you could never sing the same song.
Is there not a time for everything?
Surely a smile and a frown can never converge on the face,
Can they?
Lest they both proclaimed muscular autonomy,
As such, time will reveal all the lost and hidden treasures
That gather moth and rust,
All the harbored intentions, that deceived the eye.
Seemingly unbecoming, but already foretold in the book of life.

Momentum

Desperately trying to hold on, the wind is forced off by the moving object
The friction it creates polishes the surface, leaving a smooth finish
The wheels continue to turn,
But the locomotive that powers it rests in silence
Only the screaming wind creates a whistling sensation as the casualties increase.
Have you had a look at the occupants?
Pushing the pedal to its demise no thrust is reciprocated,
Now lightweight and buoyant, only gravity propels
That which can no longer sustain its own momentum.
...Smoking engine!
Look at the series of activities that collectively culminated in its demise.
It's hard to tell who the driver is when either of the two
Do not possess the means to steer the moving object.
The passenger's door flies open, the seat belt unfastened
And in a fraction of a second, the occupant is replaced
By the howling wind that sits in their place.
The object continues to gain momentum.
Counting the trees it passes faster than before.
Today he will fall, but before that
Shutting his eyes to reminisce of the colourfull days.
You never walk alone they say
But when perceptions diverge, and emotions go south
Is there ever any pair that still moves in one accord?
Into the wall it goes
The not-so-ductile body is condensed
As in slow motion, metal, glass, and leather congregate before its brittle form.
Let him feel the squeeze so next time it may not be repeated.

Yesterday's road trip, tomorrow's tragic headline.
And after the wreckage has been swept up,
Only the broken heart and mind
Will live to warn future generations

Aftermath

"Life goes on!"

The Promise

Every step I now take
Is like a resounding theremin
For the past heart aches that marred my path
Now crepitate beneath my feet
For every time I let go
For every time I said no
For every time I chose to move on.
A victim of heartbreak I was
Yield to their legions of devastation I did
Curling up in that lonely corner
I would surrender my heart
To undeserving Cinderellas who ripped it apart from limb to limb
Over and over again
Like a little gossip note passed down in class
But now the Rubix dilemma I have completed
And like a Phoenix from its ashes
My process of metempsychosis has planted a new endocarp
One that has overhauled the mind, body, and soul.
Inner peace has been redefined by the introspective self
And man is it good!
For it lets you appreciate the fly for its necessary evil.
The promise is simple no need for a theta
Just a jovial heart that rides the tides with no hick-up full-stop or comma
The solemn vow in my pursuit of happiness
I am the new Yes man!
And yes man il be the best that I can be
For the future wife and offspring.
For every dawn, I yawn
A fetor of past pains I'll excrete
And inspire the succulent scent of a better today
A promise to commove the psyche

Move mountains with an endearing smile
And foster glad tidings through every dose of charisma.
A promise is now engraved on my heart, a secret to the person I call myself
One that will show the way like a torch
Purging all inequities that bound my heart to the underworld
The cleansing has already begun
My heart has elected the "Me" to rule my destiny
No need to cast lots
The commission will have no omission
Neither will procrastination have a foothold
Reluctance? Maybe, but from this day forth I pitty the bull whose horns I grasp

ADVOCACY

"Often we focus on ourselves, our own happiness and self-gratification that we seldom see the pain that others are in. Open your eyes, ears, and mind and listen to the one that cries out from the deepest part of their soul"

Hopeless

...His soul is crying, but only deafening silence proceeds from his mouth
His core and inner self have all dried up,
Last night was the worst.
A great shadow emerged from the corner into the alley where he and his
mother were seated
Banqueting on discarded meals.
And descended upon them like a thick fog in a valley,
The shadow attacked!
A part of it wrapping itself around him and pressing him against the wall,
Seeping into his eyes and nostrils, rendering him disoriented,
While a greater part restrained his mother.
Aroused by her weakness the shadow went into her,
Taking turns ravaging her temple like a pack of wolves
Its death coursing through her uterus like a virus.
With no strength in his adolescent bones, he is helplessly bound up and
forced to watch
As his mother is defiled over and over again
The genocide his innocence was forced to watch,
And as quickly as it descended, it disappeared again into the thickness of
the night
Nocturnal they return from whence they came.
Crawling to her, overwhelmed by emotions he felt the piercing pain of
Watching her struggle to stay alive,
"My son!" she said "...be strong my son!" as she exhaled her last.
Since then he has never stopped crying,
Even though his tears exsiccated a long time ago.
Unmoved by the morning breeze, he continues to stare at the sun
In a world whose air is shaken and stirred by the sound of jostling
proletariats
Rushing to their slave yards and places of chores

He has never felt more alone,
Today he will venture into a store to nick a meal or two,
But the capitalist's henchmen will seize him
And devote the cane upon his flesh
The blood that trickles stands as a sign of his body's fragility
But this too will harden, just as his heart did,
Often he dreams of her, calling unto him
Asking him to join her,
But each time he reaches for her hand
The white light always takes her away…

One Dollar Plenty

'Dollar plenty boiled eggs, boiled eggs one dollar plenty eggs
Dollar one plenty eggs, you get plenty
One dollar for plenty of eggs, you get plenty
Dollar plenty eggs, one dollar plenty eggs'
...He chants this intricate mantra at the break of dawn
As he strolls down the streets
His barely covered body wearing the morning frost like a blanket
Watch as it siphons the warmth from his skin and bone
As he continues to call out...*One dollar for plenty of eggs*!!!
While others his age are in the comfort of their homes
Blanketed with parental love and overwhelmed by feasts gifts and kisses.
...he continues to call out
One dollar is plenty...I said one dollar plenty!!!
While others are driven to school
And put ink on paper about the day they will never forget
Poverty imprints deterioration marks on his face and limbs
That he may never forget every day that passes
Dollar for plenty boiled eggs...

Humanity

Cast over the edge as with ashes to a strong southern wind
Even the breeze could not help it hover. The immense weight of
rejection.
Crashing into the face of the mountain it begins to descend
Gladly welcomed by jagged edges, shrubs, and thorns
Finally landing flat on its face in a dark place it would soon call home
With a scratch, a bruise, a wound, a thousand.
Sell your brother for two pieces of silver,
Your sister for gold
Your soul for diamond
And your heart, your humanity for a lump of coal.
No party is ever despatched in search of the true treasures in life
Only for that which gathers moth and rust.
Do you remember the days of your youth?
When you broke bread together?
When you shunned evil for the glory of the light?
Now all that is left is the vessel of flesh.
Physical being with no supernatural foresight.
The love of money spawns great evil
The absence of humanity is its delight.
Repent and search for wisdom
She longs for the chance
To show you the path that leads to humanity's final resting place.
Guard your heart, for all things flow from its fountains,
Guard your heart, for without it...
What becomes of you???

Woman From Mabvuku

'Excuse me my child, do you have small small food or money to feed your mother, I am hungry.'
But like speaking to a wall her words bounce back to her
Embedding themselves in the ears concealed beneath her crotchet hat.
She gave birth to generations that neglected her generation
She gave birth to a nation that devoured her kind.
Is that her coming out of that cardboard shack
Burdened by the worn-out discoloured fabric we discard as rags?
Stitched together as they gathered moss.
Look at her gnarled sandals exposing her feet
Cracked and parched as they feed off dust and debris
Her lips, her face, engraved by the mark of her plight
Riddled with little barrows and ridges
Adding years to her age.
Is that her sitting below the tower light
Feet tucked in that dusty *goronga*
Watching the *gule* dancers move like the spirits they represent
Reflecting on past years and the children she bore
The ones that cast her aside like a peanut shell.
She is now a ghost to their success.
She clenches her fist!
One more sigh she emits
Exhaling her last
As she cradles herself in that filthy corner
The reaper has finally visited her today
And stole her breath forever
Finally, her body rests
Finally, her soul escapes
The world that defined her struggle.
She gave birth to generations that forsake her generation

She gave birth to a nation that devoured her.
Rest in peace old woman from Mabvuku.

The Brute and the Beautiful

Eyes bloodshot body itching with lust
Untamed!
Mother is not home!
You sly opportunistic fox!
...on her bed she sits
With her braided doll grasped in hand
Singing songs of little fairies and rainbows.
The door widens
And you...pounce on her innocence
forcing yourself on her
Her vulnerability you thwart like a bug
...on the edge of her bed, you leave her
Broken and defiled
And now...only 5 years old she bleeds
Beauty queen, only a year older than 16 she is
But 45 on paper you boast, if not more in age
Old cock!
Captivated by her smooth skin you choke
On your own lewd fantasies
Ones you are not even ashamed of possessing.
Disgrace!
So tease her and please her you do
With paper, And flowers,
A fragrance, A pastry,
Before you checkmate her thighs with your black bishop and rooks
Now she...with child afoot, she stands
While you...are back with your wife and friends
Coward!
Attack and flee
Destroy her life why don't you

You personified devil
She was a virgin when you met her.
She was pure when you saw her
Listen to the tears roll down her face
But the blood on the sheets is what remains
A victim
Of salacious intentions by your hand
Monster!
Is this the price paid for loving you
Colossus behemoth!
Ravaging her temple, her pride
Like a caucus
You Ogre!
That small head is not a brain!
How can you be So wicked?
She never said no
All she wanted was a ring on her finger first.
Beast!
She was a virgin when you met her
Innocent to the core
Now she is torn apart
Now she lies on the floor
Crying to the Lord for the strength to forgive the animal in you.
She was pure when you met
She was...a victim like others

About the Author

Born on January 17, 1990, in Harare, Zimbabwe, Tawanda Chitewe is a talented poet and writer who has been weaving words into verse since 2008. With a passion for storytelling and a keen eye for detail, he has honed his craft over the years, exploring themes of identity, love, culture, and the human experience.

Through his writing, Tawanda offers a unique perspective on the world, drawing inspiration from his heritage and the complexities of modern life. With a voice both authentic and evocative, he continues to captivate readers and audiences alike, solidifying his place as a rising star in the literary world.

9 798227 460844